Marie Antoinette

Library of Congress Control Number: 2018944880
ISBN 978-1-250-16882-5

Our books may be purchased in bulk for promotional, educational, or business use. Please contact your local
bookseller or the Macmillan Corporate and Premium Sales Department at (800) 221-7945 ext. 5442 or by email
at MacmillanSpecialMarkets@macmillan.com.

First published in France in 2013 by Quelle Histoire, Paris
First U.S. edition, 2019

Text: Romain Jubert and Albin Quéru
Translation: Catherine Nolan
Illustrations: Bruno Wennagel, Mathieu Ferret, Jocelyn Gravot, Guillaume Biasse

Printed in China by RR Donnelley Asia Printing Solutions Ltd., Dongguan City, Guangdong Province

10 9 8 7 6 5 4 3 2 1

Marie Antoinette

Roaring Brook Press
New York

Young Princess

Marie Antoinette was born in Vienna, Austria, in 1755. She grew up in a beautiful palace, playing in the gardens with her many brothers and sisters.

Marie's life was easy and carefree. But her country was at war with another nation: France. To help make peace, Marie's mother arranged for her to marry the young French prince, Louis.

1755–1766

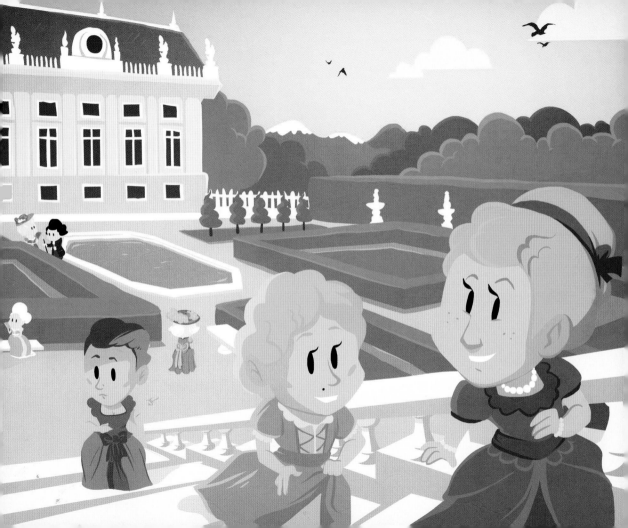

Royal Wedding

Marie went to Paris, France, to meet Louis. On May 16, 1770, they had a grand wedding. Marie was just fourteen years old. Her new husband was only fifteen.

Four years later, the king of France died. Now it was Louis's turn to be king—and Marie would be his queen.

1770

Coronation

The young couple traveled to the French city of Reims so Louis could be crowned as Louis XVI. They entered the city in a gigantic carriage. An excited crowd gathered around.

Louis was anointed with sacred oil, and the crown was placed on his head. At that moment, the French people loved Louis and his pretty wife.

The feeling would not last.

1775

Finery

Marie had always led a fancy life. Now, as queen, she insisted on the finest of everything. She bought splendid jewels and expensive clothes. She hired hairdressers to change her hairstyle every day!

She could have anything she wanted, yet Marie was not content. She found her royal duties tiresome.

___

1780

The Queen's Hamlet

Marie began to spend time away from the palace. She had a whole village built for herself, where she could spend time with her son, daughter, and friends. She called it her *hamlet*.

Marie's hamlet had a farm, so there was plenty of milk to drink and eggs to eat. Plays and music were performed by the pond to entertain the queen. Marie was never bored.

———

1783

The Revolution

Meanwhile, many people in France were poor and starving. They heard rumors about how much money the queen spent. And the king did nothing to stop her.

The people were furious. They decided to overthrow the king and queen!

An angry mob ran through the streets of Paris. On July 14, 1789, the crowd took over a government building called the Bastille.

The French Revolution had begun.

———

1789

Escape Attempt

As part of the Revolution, the royal family was forced to stay in Paris. But Marie convinced Louis that they should try to escape.

They snuck out of the city at night and reached the town of Varennes. But the postmaster there recognized the king! The royal family was arrested and taken back to Paris.

1791

Death of the King

Back in Paris, Marie and her family were thrown in the Temple prison, a dark fortress in the middle of the city.

King Louis was put on trial for betraying his country. He was found guilty. The punishment? Death.

Louis was beheaded.

———
1793

Losing a Son

Marie and her children were still in the Temple prison. She soon learned that her husband was dead. Then soldiers came for her son Louis, the royal heir. Her daughter, Marie Thérèse, would be held for two more years.

Marie begged them not to take Louis, but the soldiers would not listen. The boy was not harmed. Instead, he was sent to live with a shoemaker and his wife.

—

1793

On Trial

Soon it was Marie's turn to go on trial. She was accused of being a bad influence on the king, along with other crimes.

On October 16, 1793, Marie Antoinette was sentenced to death. She was taken through the streets of Paris on a simple cart. Then she was beheaded in a public square.

———

1793

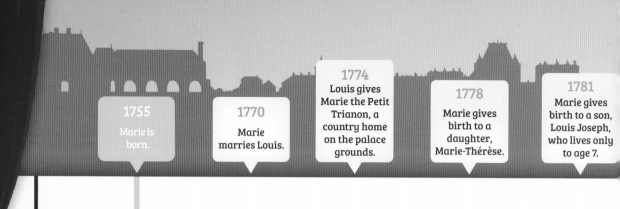

1755 Marie is born.

1770 Marie marries Louis.

1774 Louis gives Marie the Petit Trianon, a country home on the palace grounds.

1778 Marie gives birth to a daughter, Marie-Thérèse.

1781 Marie gives birth to a son, Louis Joseph, who lives only to age 7.

1740

1764 Marie's father dies.

1774 The king of France dies, making Louis king.

1775 Louis is crowned King Louis XVI of France.

1780 Marie's mother dies.

1785
Marie gives birth to another son, also named Louis.

1789
The French Revolution begins.

1792
They are thrown in the Temple prison.

1793
Marie goes on trial.

1793
Marie is beheaded.

1800

1783
Marie has her hamlet built at the Petit Trianon.

1786
She gives birth to a daughter, Sophie, who dies after less than a year.

1791
The royal family tries to escape Paris.

1793
Louis XVI is executed.

Europe in 1793

MAP KEY

1 Varennes, France

Louis and Marie were arrested here after they tried to escape from Paris during the Revolution.

2 The Terror

The Revolution became known as the Reign of Terror after its leaders arrested more than 100,000 people.

3 The Chouannerie

In this part of western France, some regions stayed loyal to the king. A civil war broke out and lasted for twelve years.

4 The Coalition

After the Revolution began, other royal families in Europe formed an army to save Louis and Marie. But their coalition was stopped by the Revolutionary army.

5 Valmy, France

Prussian troops tried to invade France on September 20, 1792. The Revolutionary army defeated them in battle near this small village.

6 Exiled Nobility

Although Marie and Louis did not succeed in leaving France, a large number of people from the royal court went into hiding in northern Europe.

French Republic

Habsburg lands, Austria

Prussian lands

Britain

Kingdom of Spain

People to Know

Louis XVI
(1754–1793)

Louis was Marie's husband and became king of France in 1774. At first, he was loved by the French people, but later they revolted against him. He was beheaded on January 21, 1793.

Maximilien Robespierre
(1758–1794)

Maximilien was a lawyer who became a leader in the French Revolution. He was behind the Reign of Terror, which killed 100,000 people. He himself ended up on the guillotine.

Marquis de Lafayette
(1757–1834)
During the French Revolution, this famous military hero tried to make peace between the people and the king. When he failed, he was forced to go into exile.

Yolande de Polastron
(1749–1793)
Also called Madame de Polignac, Yolande was the queen's close friend. She never got over the queen's execution.

....

Marie was extremely popular when she was a teenager. A crowd of 50,000 people gathered when she first arrived in France. Thirty of them were trampled to death in the chaos.

....

Some of Marie's hairstyles were almost four feet tall!

....

....

According to legend, when Marie heard that the French people could not afford bread, she shrugged and said, "Let them eat cake!" But there is no proof that she actually said this.

The people of France were angry about Marie's spending habits, but other members of the royal family were even more spoiled than she was. The king's brother wore his shoes only once. He threw a pair away every day!

Available Now

 Muhammad Ali
 Marie Antoinette
 Neil Armstrong
 Blackbeard
 Buddha
 Coco Chanel
 Charlie Chaplin

 Cleopatra
 Marie Curie
 Albert Einstein
 Anne Frank
 Gandhi
 Frida Kahlo
 Martin Luther King

 Abraham Lincoln
 Nelson Mandela
 Isaac Newton
 Rosa Parks
 Pocahontas
 Vincent van Gogh

Coming Soon

 Joan of Arc
 John F. Kennedy
 Pablo Picasso
 Princess Diana